Intersection on Neptune

Intersection on Neptune

Poems by

Donna J. Gelagotis Lee

THE POETRY PRESS

Hollywood   Los Angeles

Published by
The Poetry Press
the poetry imprint of Press Americana
americanpopularculture.com

Library of Congress Cataloging-in-Publication Data

Names: Lee, Donna J. Gelagotis, author.
Title: Intersection on Neptune / poems by Donna J. Gelagotis Lee.
Description: Hollywood, Los Angeles : The Poetry Press, [2019]
Identifiers: LCCN 2019000703 | ISBN 9780996777995 (pbk.)
Classification: LCC PS3612.E2235 A6 2019 | DDC 811/.6--dc23
LC record available at https://lccn.loc.gov/2019000703

for Dennis

TABLE OF CONTENTS

I. New York

II. New Jersey

I. NEW YORK

On the Edge of a City

As Sheepshead Bay curves into
Brooklyn, the coastal street
shimmies into town,
its flashes of light like
the glitter of a Coney Island
Ferris wheel, or the Parachute
Jump pumping its way into
the sun-cut history. I am
drenched with a Brooklyn
afternoon, like the wet-bottomed
boats floating on a slice of muted
bay. Only one sailboat
drifts to shore, seemingly
haphazard
but on course. Today, we
are just as randomly choosing
our direction, fastened
to a quick-moving city
in a lull. It is Sun-
day. It is brilliance
at work. It is a white
building shooting like a
flower to life, although the maple
and oak are leaning
towards fall,
their half-baked color
on the verge of a fantastic
catastrophe. There are many
windows casually playing
tick-tac-toe. And
even at 22 stories, a black-
winged butterfly does not
hesitate to comb the sheltered
air outside

1

our multilayered lives. We have
sprawled out. We are going on an
intentional trip, flashes of
light from bedecked and bejeweled lives
on a sensible outline of streets.

Kings Highway, Brooklyn

So you told me that kids all congregated
on Kings Highway. And you, at sixteen,
met your wife-to-be, who, at fifteen and
with her girlfriends, asked your friend Sandy
to introduce you, which he was happy to do.
And the rest was *our* story, you said.

So were the groups of kids on those street corners—
not street kids, or gangs, but kids out to meet
one another. No drink. No rough stuff.
Kings Highway was full of young people
walking up and down, grouping on corners,
kids from high school sororities and
fraternities, who'd hand out cards with the name
Delta Rho, Imperial House, Club Argyle,
Peppermint House, or Gala House.

You'd collect those cards—now musty,
fingered smudges, rubbed with a party promise
underneath. You were popular. You had
a lot of cards, sang on corners, sang at parties.
All the girls liked you, you said. And it was easy
to get a date in the early 1960s. Not to be re-
placed. Not to happen like that again. Not to save
in a bag of time. Like pennies fallen from shoes;
or money, from socks. So you told me.

Girls from All Over Brooklyn Brought Food for You

Girls in bikinis on beach blankets
    brought applesauce with chunks
    of apple in jars they kept cool
    as they waited for you on your walk
    to Brighton Beach from
    Shore Parkway to the boardwalk—
    miles of N.Y. beach, summer
    cool and a smell of suntan oil
    on the air, a slurp of soda from bottles
    you bought on the walk to the paved boardwalk
    of Manhattan Beach, where your
    teenage girlfriend sunbathed.
    You dug your feet into the sand.

Some days, you'd walk to your grandmother's
    on Coney Island, just outside of Sea Gate.
    She made you food from scratch—
    challah, sponge cake, walnut apple cake,
    her special sauce from brisket
    just for you, for dunking challah.
    She brewed you Maxwell House, topping
    it off with heavy cream.

And other days, you would climb far out on the stone jetty
    to fish, filling up your net with fluke that
    your grandma would clean and pan-fry.
    You'd buy hot dogs at Nathan's,
    ice cream on the boardwalk, knishes
    from the knish-man with coins you kept in your socks.
    From Shore Parkway to Manhattan Beach
    to Sheepshead Bay and back, you would walk,
    greeting friends and merchants who would offer you
    food. And at the beach, girls from all over Brooklyn
    were waiting with gifts prepared and wrapped just
    for you to open. They knew you were coming.
    Otherwise, the day would not be complete.

Visit

The heat in her apartment rises up
like the twenty-two
stories to her floor,
as if it radiated off the concrete
pavement, but the truth is the sun
commingles with the central heating
she flicks on. Now she is a pink buoyant marshmallow
in her big green cushiony
recliner. The heat prickles
my skin, which finds it difficult
to breathe. The humid room heaven
for the plants and flowers
we brought. She smiles
comfortably. Wool clings to my legs.
My necklace does not move
when I turn my neck. I am flushed
with politeness, wondering
if her skin has lost its
ability to withhold
body heat.
I reduce
movement to a nod of the head,
a shift of the knee.
My clothes weigh me
into the sofa.
I find the words still easy
to mouth, the larynx
flexible.
I review the ornaments
in the living room, question
their origin, although
I know I've asked before.
The cool wooden African figures
have withstood the climate
of temperature and time so well.
I review the walls, the pictures,
the untouched arrangement

of furniture. Little
has changed, only the moment
of her in her new marshmallow gown
able to negotiate the chair,
papers she wants to share, us in this room,
holding only us, these fragments of speech
and body language, even the heat,
what's particular to this day,
to be reviewed in a moment
of recall.

Solly Salamander, or Life in a Fishbowl on Avenue U

A twelve-year-old boy saw him
riotous in the water and cupped him,
placed him into a fishbowl.
At first, the boy braced the bowl before a window
at the Rosedale Hotel while he
walked the grounds and swam in White Lake,
hoping to spot teenage girls, away from their families,
hoping that he might get a glimpse of them,
of their roundness, their water eyes.

Solly swam around and around,
taking up the space in one loop, with
the lake beyond the trees before him, when
suddenly he was on Avenue U, Brooklyn.
Indian summer burrowed in.
The bowl sat on the windowsill, second floor.
The boy broke lettuce into the water before school.

Solly'd watch the mother bake herbed chicken or
order latkes, kishka, and *kasha varnishkes*
from the kosher delicatessen and then spread the food out
over the kitchen table—the boy's father widened his gait
into the room. But soon after the talk of school, news,
and neighborhood gossip, Solly'd see the buses

stop and go, stop and go, watch the girls watch the boys
who sang doo-wop on alternate street corners.
Solly swam around and around in one loop.
The boy sang songs to him, tried to imitate
the *swoosh* of the lake. But Solly could feel it pull on him,
until he jumped out of the bowl,
into the air, and out the window!
He must have thought the land had disappeared,
that with one leap he would be in the cavernous waters
of the lake at the bottom of the hill beyond the Rosedale,
swimming the depths, along with the teenage girls.

7

Prayer for Gil Hodges
—1953

It worked,
as Hodges broke out of his slump.

Who would have thought
the priest would send everyone home
with instructions to
say a prayer for the ball player?

Maybe God was a Dodgers fan
and no one knew it. But
people must have prayed hard
as the summer heat weighed down

from above. Only a hit through
the hot air would save.

The Fast

—Brooklyn, 1956

Ahead of time, your grandmother
prepared it—the large lemon.

She stuck cloves in it—
into the skin—the pungent smell

enough to wake her
if she felt faint—as she

sometimes did, at the temple
from sunup to sundown on

Yom Kippur—she wrapped the lemon
in mesh and you carried it,

ready to employ the spiced fruit
at the exact moment she might

require it—all day you stayed
with her, vigilant, patient,

such stoicism for a boy of ten—
the lemon bitter: as if the sting

would purify, cleanse the wounds
once purged of sin—but

only the aroma was required—only
the scent to jolt the senses

awake—teetering between thirst
and hunger, consciousness and un-

consciousness, belief and disbelief
dispelled—breath

and body odor weighing in like sin
until the body no longer desired—

for a brief time somewhere close
to not being—this is what

you stood guard for.

Coney Island, Thanksgiving, 1996

Boarded storefronts
silence the sidewalks.
Two policemen front
the last subway
stop, where dark
descends the alleyway.
Light bulbs glare at the street. Fear
climbs like a hungry vine.

Blocks away, your grandmother
served homemade candied
sweet potatoes, *tsimmis*, cranberry
sauce, a ribbon of challah
beside a roasted turkey,
apple pie set with her thumbprints.
You mixed soda
with seltzer from blue, silver-trigger-
nozzled bottles, rested your arms
on the monster legs
of the dining room table
to watch TV.

Now, even the ground
of the house stays quiet,
hooked to the sea,
where you flung summer fishing
lines on a slim ride
of coast, your grandmother skinned
your catch, and boys from the Bronx
took the last subway stop
to swim.

Your Father

—White Lake, c. 1955

Content in a boat.
No one has the oars
for this moment.
No one knows that there
will be few summers
to come where you
row out together
on this silver lake.

So now, here
you both are
in this photograph.
Years in sepia.
The past dulled.
But there's no
mistaking
the arms around
you, the love
that's held.
There's no
mistaking who
would be here
if he could.

Raccoon Prints
—*Harriman State Park*

Out under the stars in 1958, when you could *see* stars
and the heavens slid their milky blankets over you,

you lay on the side of a meadow rimmed by glacial
boulders, not thinking much about it at first.

You were tired. And it was so beautiful and quiet.
But the woods had their own narratives to play.

They saw you sleeping in their paths and knew
the night was long and the mountain air hypnotic

for humans. Two raccoons out for adventure thought
nothing of using you as a stepping stone, having

places to go and food to gather. Perhaps they smelled
some vague remnant of a snack but found nothing.

Perhaps they put their noses to yours for a brief second
and scurried off. They must have been surprisingly

fearless, as you were, to know the wildlife that lives
in the mountains. When dawn moved its foot, you

awakened, looked down, and quickly brushed
yourself off.

Gussie, look what the cat did!

Aunt Celia ran up to the third floor, blood covering
her head. Grandma Gussie, startled,

grabbed a towel and started to clean the darkened
red strands her house cat had made a bed,

preferring it to the towel left on the floor
for a birthing bed. Gussie'd adopted the cat,

but the cat loved Aunt Celia, who'd come
from Chicago to work, staying in one of Grandma's

second-floor rooms, one floor up from
the butcher, who'd visit, in *payot* and tzitzis,

with chicken heads for the pregnant cat that a neighbor,
who was fond of your grandmother, carried

in a basket twenty blocks, by bus, to the Parachute Jump.
The cat returned. The black-and-white cat that

followed Aunt Celia to bed. Aunt Celia returned
to Chicago and would never visit again.

Sylvia

A rose to your name when you were born.
New York sent a streetcar for you.
You and the city in company,
the skyline pure as horizon.

Your son you hoisted onto the dresser,
because you knew he could be
trusted to understand heights
and a mother's love. The dog

you bought, short and snappy,
guarding you like a miniature
mouth. Your young son taking him
out for a walk into the crisp

city air, where anything might
happen. Thanksgiving and the raw
turkey you carved into. Your son going
to pick up takeout, that November un-

like the horse-drawn–carriage days
of another age. Broadway sending
stars to your shop, when people would
come to buy stationery to write a letter.

Letters scrambling in your mind in that game
you were good at, and at the crossword puzzle
from *The Times* that no one else we knew
could do. Your card-night with the girls,

high over Sheepshead Bay. The only woman
at the casino in the Catskills on poker
night. Your son knowing where to find you.
Your smile as captivating as an ocean liner

ready to set sail. Your trip to Europe
with a girlfriend—the men in Italy
finding you hard to resist. All of the men
finding you hard to resist. All of Coney

Island laid out before you—the swing of the
Verrazano, the rumbling of the subway start,
the sailboats perpetually drifting or anchored
in a horseshoe of Sheepshead Bay. The high

building that housed you, sending you up
or down 22 floors in the shiny elevator. The terrace
straddling two rooms with a view to New York City,
beyond the Belt Parkway and the high school

you attended. I could imagine you in your girl-shoes
on the pavement, slapping your way to lessons.
Now you'd put on the coffee and tea, bring out
the rugelach, take me in as if I were your own.

There was nothing as self-contained as your co-
op apartment, with its parquet floors and
wall-to-wall carpeting, the tiny kitchen
that never felt small, the love that never felt small.

Asking us always about poetry, saving articles
from newspapers, reciting Shakespeare's
plays by heart, which neither of us could do—
saying that you liked poems that rhymed.

Tea at The Plaza
—c. 1973

Velvet roped off
the entrance.

A man in a black
suit unsnapped

the ring to the red
rope so that

we could enter.
The tables were

particular. The waiters
floated by,

linen draped
over the right arm.

I noticed they paused
beyond a partition,

presumed
they were preparing

tea.
At a nearby table,

a well-hatted woman,
dining alone, blotted red from her lips,

leaving them puckered,
as though

they had gotten used
to the feel.

Chandeliers
hung yellow light

over bulbous paintings
on the far-away wall.

At the buffet, perfect
strawberries peaked

above shimmers of crystal,
and silver spilled a cornucopia

of want to be
satisfied.

I fingered the
biscuits, then rotated

the teapot toward
me, assuming the

delicate act
of reserved

appetite.

Manhattan

A subway train vibrates
underground,
its sound the insistent
reminder of a city, its arms
those of an octopus. A
quick learner, like the mollusk,
it has a knack
for adaptation, can even
fade into the surroundings
at will, its suction cups
the many buildings taking
hold, moving the feed
to its mouth. It seems to
go great distances without
ever really leaving home.

21

In a cab,
I celebrate

my new job
with a song

aired just for me
at this moment

on 52nd street.
I savor

each block,
keeping stride

with my eyes,
the rhythm

of success
moving

through
me. First

job,
best job

I could ever
want.

The joy
of being adult

never clearer
than on this

day so full
of time.

T.S., On Stage
—Fiona Shaw, The Waste Land

As we turn the corner: the naked side
   of a building, layers of brick on bare
   wall, white-washed—*this can't be*
   Broadway, I think—the theatre one large

visible wall cordoned off,
   butting up against an adjacent
   lot, a line of porta-potties
   on the sidewalk in front.

Inside, a woman with a flashlight
   walks us down a mirrored hall
   into one of the dimmest rooms
   I've ever been in for a show.

As our eyes adjust, we distinguish rows
   of seats roped off with yellow tape,
   broken-backed chairs and dust—the air
   full of dust—and paint peeling like skin,

the belly of the theater containing us
   until we feel it and smell it
   profusely, until we feel
   uncomfortable—*do you think*
   there's asbestos? a woman in front

whispers. A bulb hangs over the stage.
   One wooden stool our focus,
   like a lame prop. And this
   is how she will use it,

the actor who will stun us into time,
   its dirt under our fingernails, the chairs
   behind us unable to hold a body,
   the floor uneven and showing nails.

We will become part of the monologue—
      like dialogue—the narrative of the past
      permeating, the afternoon flush
      against us, sighs practically visible
      in the exhale.

From a Rooftop in Brooklyn

I join the subway as it rolls
toward Coney Island Beach,
legendary stop of the 50s,
where summer was a stroll
along the boardwalk,
hot dogs at Nathan's, hands
gooey with the syrup
of a sprawling nation.

Today, a sea of brick
buildings combs
the grey air,
green parks pushing them
aside, schools still
straining to meet
the goals of a touchdown
democracy. Silver birds
cluster like butterflies
as they eagle-sweep over the
land they know, past faceless
windows, a country
below.

But from here,
the boats of Sheepshead Bay
never move,
never glide over a slate
of grey-blue, as if they were anchored
to a picture post-
card, to a time when making the best
of it was not the snaking transport
in and out of a night's
boxed lives.

Dinner at the Club

—c. 1975

You always loved waiters.
But this one lingered too long,
showed off his chest hair.
I could smell baby powder
in the air—his skin talcish
and his face double-smooth.

When the first act started—
the young woman nearly naked—I
noticed he had disappeared.
And then your exclamation—
Isn't that him?!—as he shone
in the spotlight, hand to G-string,

and I thought, *Is he going to be
bringing us our meal?*

First Trip to Brooklyn after the Attack

I'm on a condo balcony beyond Sheepshead Bay
on a hazy Rosh Hashanah Saturday. Two men in dark
suits and *payot* walk along the sidewalk, conversing

with their hands. They pull sweeping strides, and the city
takes a breath, lets its stomach out just a little.
At the table, we speak politics over turkey

and *kasha varnishkes*. Sheepshead Bay
is a wishbone. Somehow, our hearts are
steady, despite the rumbling, America

waving its flag on pickups and over
balconies as we shake our limbs
of pins and needles, and the spray

off the water wakens us, washing the air.
From here, we watch the country try on
freedom with a police presence, with

snuffed-out candles, posters of the missing.
The country manages to stretch out.
The Verrazano in the open air just a thin

line of lights, barely visible in the dusk—
and suspended, it seems.

From the 22nd Floor

As the elevator lurched upward
against gravity, the seconds tumbled
like small pieces of fruit. In
the hallway, as polished as a hospital,
the dominoes of common doors. And over yours
your abbreviated name. We teeter
above Brooklyn—the Verrazano to the left,
the Empire State: center, Sheepshead Bay
to the right—high over Brighton Beach, in a building
of Russians and Jews. In the lobby,
a sign doubles in Russian. Residents each know
the wait for the lift
as it pulls upward—up over a city.
From here, we can see
the mouth of the country—used
to change. We no longer speak
of the missing Twin Towers as we watch
the July fireworks drop starbursts
along the water. The long ride up.
The long ride down. The long streets
you walked as a boy now dim
with block-like buildings.
The lights inside point
to each detached life, at night,
when the streets fill with darkness,
and with no accent of any kind,
except on this holiday, with popping sounds.
We look for gunshots. But the streets
are empty. They are far
beneath us.

Intersection on Neptune
—Neptune Avenue, Brooklyn

The sea smell rushes
in on a sudden breeze, like
that vehicle that veers into the space
just as someone pulls out. Older
couples, hearty Jamaicans,
Yiddish accents; land of immigrants;
watch them claim it—
Chinese, Russians, ladies with thick
jewelry, men with yarmulkes;
the elderly line up at the strip
mall to trade stories, their props
canes and old-world hats. Yellow
cabs turn the corners. Yellow
lights let you cross only to the island.
Sirens interrupt talk. The sea breeze inter-
venes. The walk to the boardwalk is short.
But here, at this intersection, we
have gathered, where the city turns.
And we find a parking space,
crowded, a little tight, but afterwards
it's enough; we all fit.
We smell the sea, the kosher bakery.
Our house is a high-rise.
Our horizon, the Verrazano and the Empire
State. We're on the finger
of New York City—the end
of the subway line, or the beginning—
the city starts and ends here,
on the country's pivot point.

II. New Jersey

What's American?

When people in the neighborhood broke
the window of Grandfather's store, with his name
in Russian—he changed the name to something
American, put up another window,

and swept up bits of glass in the dust.
His children were not allowed to speak Russian.
Yet he and Grandmother whispered it between them.
And the Orthodox priest came over with carolers each Christmas.

In the yard, the chickens clucked. Grape vines grew.
And by evening, after he closed the store, Grandfather drove
down the streets of the neighborhood with produce
unsold that day. Everyone knew him. Everyone called

him by his American name. Maybe it was because
it was the Depression that they broke his window.
But I doubt it. Grandfather had the only store in the neighborhood.
People brought their stamps for food.

Suffering was *here* now.
Did they feel he had to feel that too?
Did their anger unleash on the old country or the promise
of finding something better in the new? Hunger

swung on a vine. Their tongues tasted bitterness.
Grandmother remembered her own hunger
and dropped free candies into the bags of customers as they left.
She pounded her fist into the dough for the bread to rise.

Everyone wanted the bread to rise. Women wanted to make the bread
to eat. In her first days in America, Grandmother stirred pots in a hot
restaurant in NYC. Hungry, she asked for *khleb*. "Say *bread*," her boss
said as Grandmother tasted her tears, salty in her mouth. "Say *bread*."

Between Two Women

In the bedroom just off the stairs,
the midwife ensures a safe birth.
Your sister, only ten years old, is sitting

on the front porch, waiting to see you—
new sister to six, five siblings still residing
in the two-story house with the grocery store,

the Coca-Cola sign like promise in the window.
The midwife, a friend of your mother.
Their husbands, workers at the steel mill

years ago. On visits, she joins your mother
in the kitchen. Both women exchange Russian,
their hands in the vegetables for borscht, *golubtsi* . . .

Words fly out, quick, deliberate, with no room
for dalliance. An apple needed is one needed now.
Cherries asked for are cherries to be plucked off

the tree before hands finish the dough, rolled out and
pinched perfect. Hair pulled back. The mind strong,
like steel. Yet between these women changing paths

in the kitchen, beyond—the orchard, there must have
been some re-laxing, the mind as busy as the hands
yet distracted, as though they were working over

the lands of their births, the limbs of the cherry trees
undulating in full bloom among the persistent
apple trees of these united states.

Hunger and Money

Mother was born just months before Black Tuesday.
Now four, she was a child of the Great Depression.
But you wouldn't know it. She looked from the inside

out, but not as children did whose parents held relief
stamps, who gazed at the candy counter with hunger
on their breaths. She snuck in when no one was there,

took a piece of candy, and chewed it in a corner of the store
her father owned, *she* owned, so it was okay.
Her mother would slip a piece of candy into the hands

of children when her father was working the deli counter.
It was like a gift, as parents' lost jobs floated in the air
on magic carpets. Someone in a bank was up there and

someone who sold off all that stock, hoping to get it back.
Her mother watched the men and women come in as years
etched into their faces. Her father was glad people got relief

so that they, and he, could eat, though with chickens
and grape vines and cherry trees, with a vegetable garden
that grew enough to sell as well as eat, it was doubtful that

his children would hunger. Her mother made chicken soup
from scratch each Sunday. Her father brought in the eggs.
Cherry soup was her mother's Ukrainian specialty.

And her father liked his Russian borscht. Fruit made drink,
which the local priest loved, kept behind the Virgin Mary,
where they went to pray. Mother would hide and watch.

She was young, the youngest. And everyone thought
she was too small to understand. But she saw how hunger
and hope intertwined. She saw necessity in a dollar

and in a coin. Work was a luxury, valued, like gold.
She swung the door open to the grocery store. She learned
its workings. She sat aboard the Model T her father drove

after he closed shop for the day to sell what had not been bought.
Everyone knew him, addressed him by *Mr*. Everyone was just
looking to climb out of the hole a lot of speculation had dug.

At the military institute, c. 1945,

where her new dad had run track,
there used to be a place
where the athletes met afterward
to smoke. It was all okay
in those days when cigarettes
were cool and GIs smoked abroad—
we even sent them cigarettes!

In the movies, love and strength
and loneliness were linked to cigarettes.
But why the boys looked forward
to puffing away with lung-smoke had
something to do with friendship
and acceptance, and then the nicotine
gave a high not similar to a running

high, but a high just the same. What ex-
citement in a special place at a special
time, when the body was discovering
how far it could go without running
out of breath. The beautiful future
officers grooming themselves for
the unclear distance looming.

Her new dad, so young and forward looking,
digging in at the start and pushing off.

Eggs
—*Elizabeth, c. 1948*

He'd have to be careful.
One false step and everything could
come crashing down. He loved his job. He drove
a truck, picked up cartons, delivered them
to neighborhood stores. There were a lot of
farmers in Elizabeth. You'd never know it now.

He could smell grass and dew and egg-
shell, translucent as morning at dawn.

He flung
the door open to his truck, carried armfuls
of fresh-packed egg crates. He drove
through the early hours, when promise
was as golden as an egg yolk or a sunrise,
when the chickens would push forward the day
the way each person meant to, giving what
could be given and going on to the next business.

He Built the Turnpike

At Elizabeth, he drove a flatbed they'd
load those houses on that were in
the way and torn down. They were bits
of scrap now, piles of boards and timber,
shingle and brick, all to pave the way
for the big highway. He hurried in, watched
the men load the lumber turned trash.
If someone's dream had been there, you
couldn't see it in the remains. It was all
about what was coming, what was streamlining
the state and country. The past was a broken
mirror, and no one could see his reflection.
Clear out. Mow a path. Cut it down.
The future had no patience. There were cars waiting
on side streets. Hurry. Build quickly.
Before you know it, a sea of asphalt will lick
through the Garden State. You'll have to pay
to drive this. He built the turnpike, part of it,
near Elizabeth, which turned out to be
its heart, well paced and smooth.

In First Grade

Penmanship was important.
So was recess and naptime.
We each had a pencil case.
There was a sharpener in the back
of the room. You'd crank one end
after you put the pencil in the other
end. As you turned the metal lever,
shavings would collect inside the small
barrel that someone would have to
empty. The teacher would print letters
on the board with chalk, large enough
for us to see them. They were beautiful,
and clear for us to copy. If you pressed too hard,
you'd break the pencil point and have to go
to the back to sharpen it. But if you were smart,
you'd check those pencils before class and sharpen
them ahead of time. Because soon you'd open
your black-and-white notebook and fill in the lines
with loops and lines and periods. If your printing
was very good, you might get a star shining
in glitter at the top of your page. It would never
be so simple again to be as neat and patient
with your efforts, to know that if you wrote
precise letters, it would make a difference
in how people would look at you
as they read what you so intently meant.

Saying Penance

—c. 1967

The panel slid over with a thump.
Which priest did God choose for me?

I kept trying to see, even as I spoke, but then a voice
sterner than God's pronounced my penance.

I left the box, hurried to the pew, crossed myself.
Why did he give me ten (!) Hail Marys?

I had to get back home, ride my bike with my friend,
listen to records. Next time I'll come early, wait

to see which priest enters which box. I'll
stand in the line that's faster, listen to the voice

that's softer, say a few Hail Marys—that's
all I'll have to do.

When God Made Babies
—c. 1966

Babies were miracles. On TV, storks carried them
to expectant mothers. Babies were from heaven.
You could tell that by looking at their angelic
faces or by watching the priest pour water

onto their heads. You'd need a godmother
and a godfather, who'd step in for the real
mother and father should anything not
from heaven happen to them. When God

made babies, they were born good, sort of.
Still, they had to be baptized. God loved
babies, we were told. That's why he made so
many. That's why you got married, so he could

give you one or, if you were lucky, more.
So you had to be good. So you might get
a baby delivered to you sometime in the night.
How one day you would discover the surprise.

Even if you'd planned it, you couldn't be sure
you'd be blessed. It was like a test, this baby
thing. As kids, we really didn't understand it.
We didn't spend a lot of time thinking

about where we came from. We didn't even care
that much about babies. They were something
we weren't. And we weren't going back there,
wherever that was.

Daisies

You wanted to pick daisies
from the field down the street, which was half-
wild and overgrown. Your mother would smile that mother-smile.
And dawn would be a field of daisies.
It would take so little to make her happy.

1939 would turn food to the table. Children were skipping again. Fathers
   were buying bread.
People were dreaming of Oz land. But another war stood on the
   cobblestone precipice.
Two sons, brothers would join. Both would come home.

Years later, we picked daisies, put them in jars, you say. I don't
   remember that. But you add,
They looked so pretty.

I picked daisies for you in roadside fields. They were wild,
like weeds, and free.

What We Knew Then

Curlers worked.
An open window let in flies.
It was cool after a summer rain.

It was hot in summer, and you sweat.
After it rained, you could collect night crawlers in the yard for fishing.
Punks kept away mosquitoes.

Kids walked to school.
You could jump into a pile of raked-up leaves.
The bad kid in the neighborhood might beat you up if you weren't
    careful.

The pond we skated on in winter had thin spots.
A piece of cardboard worked as a sled on the snow.
Girls couldn't wear pants to school.

The milkman delivered before you got up.
We wandered farther than we were told we could go.
A neighbor would sometimes tell your parents.

The government was mostly right.
The lake we swam in had sink holes.
Everything was going to get better.

In Sixth Grade

I was in the schoolroom at the end
of the building that jut into the edge
of the woods beside a field we used
to play handball in. In the forest were
trails that spilled out right at the end:

I'd daydream into those woods
on a pony brought for carnival
that no one else knew how to ride.
I'd mount that pony correctly
and head there. The trail would go
for miles, past one sweeping branch
after the next. I'd have to duck to

avoid getting hit, socked in the face
by one of those branches, with the
swoosh of teacher's ruler come
smashing down on the desk
at the front of the room,
where I should have been looking.

I'd learn to look, daydream
while gazing directly
at the teacher. I could even smile.
Because by test time, I'd answer correctly
every question presented. I had been on
that trail, had ridden miles through the woods,
and had come out on the other side
with a leaf in my mouth.

Model Horses

You can buy them from a catalog,
collect them from a hobby shop.

Why play with dolls when you can
have horses, large ones with cobalt

eyes, Palomino ones, Appaloosa ones?
They can gallop in your dreams

at night, leap into the classroom
when the teacher drones on about

states you have to learn. You can put
a horse in every state and follow

it to borders. And when it comes
to rest in your dreams, you can imagine

the grand pastures you'll ride in
and the many acres you'll cover.

No one will understand why you continue
to add to your collection.

Maybe just one more will lead you
to where the horses have been all along.

In the Neighborhood

Our Cape Cod, on the corner,
faced the main road, where
occasionally a cat was hit, its

body limp on a shovel that a parent
used to carry it to a homemade grave
in a backyard. Hedges would

bar youngsters from the street.
Kids had to be visible to a mother,
who'd allow them to play only

in a backyard or to sled down
the slope to the sidewalk in winter.
Mothers didn't know who

would be driving by on the main road.
But nearly everyone who turned
onto a side street either lived

in the neighborhood or was visiting someone
there, as if that connection were enough for us
to forget to be cautious.

The Dogcatcher

The dogcatcher came with his long noose
at the end of a pole he wrapped his gloved

hands around should he have to hold
the dog and risk getting bitten. He heaved

the dog into the back of the truck, screened
off from the front, and the dog would often

whimper, the dog we were all afraid of.
Dogs without collars were a target

for the dogcatcher. Dogs with tags would be
taken home. Dogs in the dogcatcher's truck

rode to the dog pound and after a time
were euthanized if no one came to adopt

them, which was often the case. The dogcatcher
was a big man with few words. He came

to catch a dog and take it away.
He came to answer the calls.

Over the Bridge to Seaside
—c. 1968

Our car rolled over the bridge, white caps visible through the gaps at the height. With the windows rolled down, I could feel the spray off the bay on my arm, smell its low-tide marshes. I felt as if I could almost reach the fishing boats rocking in the bay, crab traps tied to their benches.

At the boardwalk, we mounted hand-painted horses—cotton candy and the salty breeze on our lips. Children playing at the edge of the water, digging with plastic buckets and building towers of sand. Teenage boys called out numbers, tempted us to give up our coins.

The cackles of gulls settling on the air, with the breaking of waves. The laughter of children let loose, with all that possibility.

Place

You can see the window to my bedroom from the main road
out front. When I was growing up, it was hidden by trees and shrubs.
Tulips grew along the side of the house. A long plot of land
separated us from the neighbors, who had a similar Cape Cod:
two bedrooms downstairs, a large attic up; ours, converted

to a third bedroom. There was just one bathroom for the entire house.
It was outside my bedroom and between mine and my parents',
which you never entered without knocking. Inside were treasures:
Mom's jewelry box, two dressers with folded clothes, an ivory brush
next to a vanity mirror. At the vanity, Mom would brush my hair

while I was sitting there and I'd imagine what it would feel like to be
grown up. The kitchen was in the back of the house, beside my bedroom.
I never thought about it, but the oven was catty-corner to my room
and the refrigerator held up the wall behind the headboard of my bed
that my pillow rested against, where my lips swelled three times the size

one night after a bug flew into my mouth while I was riding home
on my bicycle from my best friend's house. It was dusk. I spit it out
and forgot about it. It must have bitten me. That's what they said
in Emergency, where Mom drove me late that night after I knocked
on her door with my hand over my lips. Still, I went back to sleep

in that room, pulling the sheet up to my lips as if to stop another bug
from finding them. There was a second window on the other
side of my room, the long side that the bed pushed against,
beneath the pine tree, which had a needle-bed
and mostly kept the rain out. It was so big it smelled like

a pine forest when you opened that window. But the other open
window smelled like earth (especially when it was sunny) and snow
after a snowfall. It smelled like wood and house and bushes. I could
see only the neighbors' house (I wouldn't stare) and the tulips if I leaned
out the window. Sometimes a cat would be lying in the tulip bed.

It was all my own, this corner of the house of the lot we lived
on. I couldn't hear the main road, what with all the shrubs and hedges.
I tried to help cut them once with the clippers. The clippers were large
and sharp and too heavy for me. My arms were tired before one bush
was done. And bugs would jump out onto my arms. It was hot,

and I sweat, and little gnats stuck to my skin. I had to hose off
afterwards with the hose on the side of the yard near the
street, where the garden was, with a rosebush and more tulips
and carnations. The hose was beside the kitchen door. We'd water the
    flowers
every day in summer. I think there were daffodils too. I remember
    daffodils.

Zeal

In junior high school, my knees
turned red on the walk to school—

numbed or tingling skin, in winter,
because of a dress code.

Someone must have come to
her senses, as by ninth grade

the code was dropped. Pants.
The girls wore pants. But I was

already kindred. I knew it was
different to be a girl—and that

difference tagged along. Tolerance.
And pain—a monthly reminder

since elementary school. I didn't need
winter to tell me. I didn't

need a dress to prove
I was female. I bit the air.

Even today I can feel my body
quiver, my skin red, a question

abiding on my tongue as adolescence
pushed forward with incredible zeal.

The Women in the Neighborhood

Our neighbor had a clothes dryer.
        Her husband knew how to hook it up.

The rest of the women hung clothes outside
        even in winter. Their hands cracked

with cold. The pants froze
        stiff. And the clothespins would rust.

The women in the neighborhood had washing machines
        and irons and ovens. Mothers made lunches

and packed them in paper bags or lunch boxes with cartoon
        characters that kids took on the bus to school.

The women cleaned and cooked and washed
        and ironed and shopped. And then

some went to work. The women in the neighborhood
        lived in Cape Cods. They used

curlers and had backyards with above-ground pools
        if they were lucky. If they worked, they earned

more freedom, as they were paid and they could buy
        whatever their husbands agreed to.

Record Player

Drop, drop the needle down
precisely at the beginning
of the song. Do it gently so
that it doesn't skip, and scratch
the record. At the end of the song,
when you hear only static, pick up
the arm and place it onto the cradle.
A few crackles will be part of the song.

You knew how old a record was by how
much static there was, or if the needle
skipped. You could hold the record up to
the light to see any scratches. It was easy
to bend a record. That's why you took it
out of the sleeve by the edges, balanced it
between the fingertips of each hand, as if
you were giving a gift, because records were precious.
There were collections of records. People borrowed
records. There were record stores in practically
every mall and in most towns. Sometimes, an album
would have the lyrics printed on the cover or on a piece
of paper inside. An album cover was often a large photo.
It told you something of the songs or the singer or the group.
You could gaze at the cover when you listened to a song.

Pulling an album from your collection was like giving yourself
a treat that promised more. Albums made money — sometimes
lots of money. You could even sell yours or trade it. Stores
would buy your albums. But you would usually keep them
for years. And one day you would play one and be transported
back to who you were many years before, to where you were,
and, possibly, with whom. You would feel it in your body.
Once a record was in your hand, it was only a matter of motion,
a series of steps: slipping the record out of the sleeve, placing it on
the turntable, checking the needle with your fingertip, and placing
the arm down to hear the low crackling before the first notes.

Replenishing the Past

In Trenton
        there was a five-and-dime.
We'd take the bus into town, sit
        down at the counter, the smell of brewed
coffee over aisles of plastic items like a new
        America. I never could see

the end. We'd dropped the bomb,
        and the world feared us.
I wondered if I would grow up to be
        a counter girl, but Mother whisked
me away, back into the street, where I was
        too busy for such fantasy.

I wish I could replenish the past
        with a hormone, time
like a heartbeat. But here I am
        in suburbia. My life like that photograph
I took in another country, cobblestone
        underfoot, the slippery past
catching me off balance.

For the Love of Country

Within a mile of home were three
stables. Though development
squeezed them in, we found them.

We rode our bikes there. We rode
the horses there. Our parents had
ridden there. So it was almost

a right, our connection
to the land that was disappearing.
Travel a few miles farther

and there was another,
even larger, stable, where nearly
everyone had ridden. Was it because

our ancestors rode that we
longed to discover on horseback?
How I'd love to hose down

the horses, their muscled bodies,
muzzles to the ground,
earth at their nostrils all day,

the sun on their backs, tails
swatting the flies away. I'd have
a horse in my backyard if I could.

I'd feed him out the window.
I'd tie him to the pine tree,
ride him to school. Didn't kids

do that not so long ago?
Now school buses and cars cover
all those roads that swipe suburban

neighborhoods, where the horses grazed
as they longed to run. Big
country, what are you doing to

the horses? Why do we no longer feel
the need to ride, the horse at our calves
and thighs, the reins in our hands,

the open country promising us
dreams we didn't even know
we had, when we were less distracted?

What I would give for the smell
of horses, the oiled leather, the pasture
covered with dew, the forest at dusk

when the sun has shimmied
into the trees and the moon is wanting
for me to find the way, suddenly.

It Happened in Trenton

Feeding the ducks at Cadwalader Park.
Shopping at Lit Brothers.
Stopping at the Woolworth's soda fountain counter.

We'd take the bus home,
make an appointment to
go to "doctors' row." We'd

visit the Barracks from school,
stop at the information desk at
the Trenton Public Library.

We'd drive to the Trenton train
station to travel to New York
or Philly or D.C., assured by

the lot attendant we could
come back late safely. We'd eat
steaks with the men in

suits at Pete Lorenzo's,
dine in Chambersburg,
go for a burger at Rossi's.

We'd see performances, or dance ourselves,
at the Trenton War Memorial. We'd take
the "Trenton Makes" bridge. We'd

eat Trenton pork roll, play
at the State Fair, in Trenton,
say confession at Holy Angels

Church, pray at St. Raphael.
We wouldn't be afraid to drive
through the city, except for maybe one

or two streets, and then there would be
police nearby to protect us. Our parents
lived in Trenton. Families gathered on

porches, boated on the river, exchanged
news at the neighborhood grocer, picked
up bread and donuts on sale at the Wonder-

Hostess shop. People had cherry trees in
Trenton, and grape vines for wine. There were
chicken coops and all kinds of vegetable

gardens. Hucksters would peddle door-to-
door. And church would center
a community. Your house could get blessed

in Trenton.

Conception

Such a sudden step off the street
in Trenton, as if one *needed*
to have faith. And how much

easier is it in a sanctuary,
where barely a whisper is heard
and daylight filters through images,

all sound an echo of reverence?
Surely your prayers will be heard.
Even if you never face the priest—

and don't you *not* want to?—
even if you refocus your thoughts
when you return to the outside

world where you live, for this
brief alteration in the time
you spend or save or lose,

some aspect of the light enters
as you connect to what you
may not have been sure existed.

The lake, when I was growing up,

smelled of pine and briny water,
rocked us in rowboats when we set
the anchor down.

People swam in that lake though
you couldn't see the bottom.
It was carved out of the woods,

in forest at the edge of the Pine
Barrens. The roads leading in
were sand, as if the ocean

tried to get there, or once
was there. None of us really
liked to get into the rowboat.

It was crowded, and we sat in a row
on benches. But once we were out
on the lake, its vastness seemed to

swallow fear and all memory of it,
the dark heart of the lake
beneath us. The sky opened up

as if trying to give us passage.
The trunks of pines needled upward
out of the sand. And other lakers

would motor past us and wave,
as if they had met us before. Yet
we all wanted to get back on land

in the end. Even Mom and Dad were
happy to feel the earth's support. And we'd go
running to Uncle's house, where Aunt

would bring out the crabs and we'd watch
as the men dipped them into the boiling
water, as if a rite of passage. We'd forget

everything when it was time to eat, but
could smell, every so often, when someone
moved, a hint of damp pine clinging to skin.

It was this scent that would stay in our nostrils,
to be recollected as we passed among the thick
pines stuck in the sand, the wood-framed screen door

slamming back as Aunt went to dump out the sand
and hang our suits on the line. The two-room house
with cots and pullouts for sleep. But there was little

sleep, though we were tired. The crabs steamed. I
couldn't watch as they fell into the pot, turning red
and still, the rest clawing over the bucket, grabbing—

with their strong claws we ate—the handle of the bucket
or someone's finger. It didn't hurt, we were told. It was quick.
Still, they seemed to know this was not the sea. They seemed to

tell one another, and one was getting away. *Run,* I thought. *Run.*
There is the door where the wood swings, and you can smell
the pine, and there is sand on the rim. I could kick open the door.

You could claw your way back.

Birthday Cake

Mom would put the record on.
And kids from school who were
invited ran around the chairs
until the music stopped, and

quickly sat down. Someone wouldn't
get a chair. You wouldn't want it
to be you. It was a popular game.
We called it musical chairs,

as if the chairs were musical,
which they weren't. They
were fold-up chairs we kept in
storage in the basement. We

never played much down there.
In winter, it was cold and damp.
And that's where the washer was
and, probably, dirty laundry.

Mom had to lug the wet clothes up
the stairs and out to the back clothesline.
I never did it, but they must
have been heavy, which leads

me to baking cakes, which
involved carrying cake pans, lining
them with waxed paper you'd
cut from a roll to fit. We had

a mixer, so that wasn't hard,
and we got to lick the beaters. Cake
baking smelled good. Our whole
house smelled sweet. You knew

a good day was coming if a cake
was in the oven. That's why
I leave my oven filled with old pans.
Though I'll never bake cakes

like that. I'll not beat a flour and
sugar and artificial-ingredient mix.
It's far easier now
to buy a cake.

Two Bridges to Brooklyn

The first hoists the highway up on stilts only

to let you down again,
more highway than bridge.

The next pitches into the sky
unmistakably, striking

into the horizon miles before
you arrive. Weighted

into the bay, suspended
on the muscle of twentieth-

century workers, my stepfather's
story of walking the catwalk

without a safety belt.
How each of us now traverses

this ponderous bridge
as confidently,

as though nothing
could fail, as though

we have already made
the connection between

where we were and where we
are going. And these bridges

will hold us so briefly
we will hardly notice

the space between
the reaches of land.

Driving Donner Pass in the 1960s

You knew about the danger,
the story of a wagon expedition
that fell to the claws of a blizzard
and was consumed. But you drew
America on your 18-wheeler across
the country and were headed up there.

The roads were as slick as history, maybe
slicker. So you pulled off for the night.
The owner walked you to your cabin.
"Does it have heat?" you asked. And he motioned
to the logs at the foot of the bed, a promise
to be warm at Donner Pass. The road waited

for daybreak so that you could see where to go.
What lurked on the side roads, on paths
others wouldn't venture to now? You had delivered
the freight and were headed back. Though the road spun
round with no guardrail, you were going
to make that drive and survive.

Wine, and Jewish Rye in Bacon Fat
—c. 1939

When I was nine, I'd go out on Saturday
to buy Jewish rye bread
at the bakery a block away.
Uncle brought the bacon, and
pork for the sausage he used to make in the basement
with Grandpa. Each Sunday, at breakfast, Uncle
fried up the Jewish rye in bacon fat
and served it to me with a glass of wine.

He'd been an officer
in the Prussian Army. I attended
military school. But summers I
spent two weeks on Uncle's farm.
I'd have to clean the chicken coops, but
we went swimming and fishing in
the brook. I caught a lot of trout but
didn't eat any. Didn't like fish.

Uncle, who raised pigs, would slaughter
a sow and bring the meat back to our
house. He and Grandpa prepared the sausage
in the basement. First thing on
Sunday morning, Uncle would march
into the kitchen. He was commandant
over the stovetop. The bacon would sizzle,
crisp as a salute.

Neighborhood Grocer

—*Trenton, c. 1939* –

They'd come with food stamps and
leave with eggs, milk, flour, vegetables. Sometimes
he would give them cigarettes, or some potatoes from
his backyard. "Here Mrs. Jones"—he'd address each Mr.
or Mrs. "Take a little something extra," he'd say, dropping
a freebee into her bag. She would thank him and
always come back. He wouldn't stop working—in
the store all day, loaded up the truck in the evening
with leftover produce and drove around the neighborhood,
greeting people door-to-door. At night, he'd
weed the garden. At dawn, he'd gather eggs
from the coops in the yard. Customers would
call him Mr., his wife Mrs., when they saw her,
which was once in a while. And she would always
try to give something for free, a piece of candy,
fruit. Sometimes the sons would help deliver groceries
after school. They would not stay in the store.
That was their father's as much as the trees and the grapes and
the ground he tended. As much as the cellar where
he kept jars his wife packed, some with coins.
When he passed on, his wife would take
over the store. But before then, he would be there,
dressed in a suit and vest, even while sweeping up.
He handed out flyers he'd write up with the week's
produce and prices. Usually, if a customer came
into the store and didn't see him, he'd be in the freezer, a big
walk-in freezer that you wouldn't want to close the door to by accident.
Or he'd be restocking the candy counter. His youngest daughter
liked to run into the store, take a piece of candy
when no one was looking. It was a game, like hide-and-seek. She
could always take candy. They'd start to call for her, and she'd appear.
The candies were wrapped and colorful. The kids in the neighborhood
liked the candy counter, with its large windows they could press against,
trying to see the candies. Her father would give them a grab bag
for a penny. Her mother would give a piece of candy to a child
who was hungry. She'd cook soup and take it to neighbors

who were sick, while her husband was busy in the store.
By the time the century turned, the lot had grown smaller.
Three plastic chairs waited on the side porch.
Now, would people know their neighborhood grocer?
Would passersby hear, on reaching the corner door
where two streets meet, the faint sound of Mozart
coming from the parlor, the owner sweeping off
the steps that lead up and into the store?

The Earth's Provision

How we loved a summer rain that cooled,
    brought the grass to smell green,

night crawlers rising up hours early, our feet cool
    on the concrete path to the porch,

where we sat watching the rain drench
    the earth—summer

brief as youth, now dormant in
    the mind—hold me on the front porch.

Give me a bowl of ice cream
    as I dream of the earth in bloom,

wet as a kiss—watch me
    lick the spoon—completely satisfied

at the world to explore—
    how the rain beads on the holly

bush and the maple flashes red-
    violet—see how far our toes

go in the puddle catching bursts
    of sunlight—no wonder

we believed in heaven—no wonder
    we could see the stars at night

as the smell of the earth filled our
    lungs, and no one would question

how far we had come—no one doubted
    the earth's provision.

The Box with the Phone

Everyone knew where the pay phone was —
on the street, at the beach, at the mall,
in a department store, outside the local
pharmacy, at the movie theatre or drive-
in. One line to the world, if you had a
coin. Or maybe you could find one,
or several, if you pressed the coin-return
lever. If you were lucky, change would come
tumbling down. That's how kids found
money for candy. You could hear the sound
if someone hit the jackpot. Neighborhood kids would
check the coin return, sliding a finger into the smooth slot
beneath the little trap door in case someone forgot
the change. Strangers would check coin returns, sometimes
ask you for a dime to make a call.

You knew you were on your own when you left home
until you could reach a phone booth.
If someone broke down on the road, cars would stop
because of the white flag on the antenna, though
you could never be sure who would stop. Mothers
didn't want daughters to drive at night. Most people,
however, were nice. Still, one never knew
what could happen on the road. An operator
might answer if you couldn't get through.
She could make the call for you.
She was pleasant. You felt as if you had
a friend if you could reach an operator,
wherever you were.

People would call phone booths — to look for someone
or just to see who would answer. You
had to be careful if you decided to answer the phone.
There were doors, and it was warmer inside in winter
but sometimes too hot in summer. There was a phone book
attached to a ledge with a chain. There were often pages missing
and numbers circled. There was a pen if you were lucky,

but most of the time it was gone. You'd have to cup
your hand around the mouthpiece if anyone was waiting to use
the phone and you didn't want that person to hear. At times,
someone would get impatient and knock on the door. You'd
have to raise a finger for "just a minute." I used to love
phone booths. They were so private: little enclosed glass boxes.
With a door that'd fold open. Sometimes I'd pick up the phone
and pretend someone was on the other end.

Paul

always sat at the head
of the table,
near the window,
in an Arrowback chair.
Or he was outside
at the barn, working
on his tractor, or
in the field, wrapping
up the hay bales.
His wit was quick.
His comments, straight
and blunted. He had
a laugh that was deep-
hearted. You knew what
he meant. I heard him
tell the young boy he would
fall through that floor
if he kept jumping.
And the boy's eyes
popped open wide as he
stood still for a moment,
looking at the older man,
and then sat down. Paul liked
to pull on his wife's tales:
Ah, Tess, is that how it was?
And he was gentle with friends,
his voice the calm of a wheat field.
He grew up in Amish country
and was as sturdy
as the support beams in the house he built.
He would give you anything from
the freezer downstairs if you would
agree to go get it.

Contemplating Summer in New Jersey

Now summer,
moisture
dripping from
our foreheads, the
breeze bringing coolness
off the trees
or, better yet,
the sea, whose
salty lick is
rough yet
delicious, though
driving there
without air
conditioning
can be brutal.
Better to take
a country road,
the sweet oak and elm
releasing fragrance,
the twisted roads
passing cow pastures
and horse farms. Did
I say that you would
soon forget where you
needed to be so quickly,
for that's the purpose
of summer, now having
done its job, now sitting
back on a lawn chair
where you should be
reading a book with
some lemonade sold
by the neighborhood
children in front of their
house with the parents

looking on? Did I tell you
how it once was
for children, riding
their bicycles up and
down the sidewalks
freely, swimming
in the local watering
hole, drying off in
the summer sun, tasting
how fresh the water
was, how drying the heat,
rolling marbles down
the pavement, buying
ice cream from the
ice cream man in his
singing truck, everyone
singing in summer in New Jersey?

A Good Area

We no longer want to see the conductors
of our electricity. Move them
underground. The stars are faint.
We don't search the sky anymore.

Step around the glass in the street.
Watch out for black-legged ticks.
The bridge to the park is electrified.
You feel the hairs on your arms.

You think—each neighborhood has
its drawbacks. The street sags
like belly fat. To the left
is a dead end.

A boy tries a tricycle
in front of high-tension lines.
The quiet road develops
a raucous personality.

Highways strangle tracts
of land. Houses pop up
with their eyes bulging.
The road leads out

and back. South to north. And
north *is* south. Where we are,
a geographic pacifier. Crime steals
property values. We don't want

security systems. Drive up hills
to railroad tracks—passenger trains,
freight trains? Noise like a drumroll.
My heart rumbles in the Northeast Corridor.

And so we rush. To feel our breath
or to lose it to catch it. The houses crowd close.

73

We look for land untangled
by high-tension wires.

We don't want to hear the whistle
as winter bares the field,
clears the land to the area
where we will live.

Ball Game
—Hamilton, 2002

Night lights flood the newly groomed
field as players tag runners,

catch fly balls,
dig up dirt as they slide to home

at the ball field where my father,
who co-founded the league,

would not have dreamed I'd be,
trying to know him before divorce was common,

mentioned casually by kids who divide time
between parents as well as sports.

Now teens reach for their gear
with practiced precision, find

their place on the field without assistance,
as if they owned the field and the dugout and the new

clubhouse with the loudspeaker and the rules,
and the calls the adults argue . . . the calls they'll argue—

brilliance: the smack of the ball in glove,
against bat, the touch of home base.

Circa 1968 Auction
—*Trenton*

Each horse was led into the circle.
The handler was a man. The auctioneer
was a man. The buyers were men. Everyone
bidding was a man, though women and girls were
present. And I thought, *Could this be my horse?*
The chestnut had a slight limp.
The Appaloosa, a sway back. The bay
was handsome but wiry, nipping at
the lead shank. I had not enough money,
no farm, no stall, no pasture.

Some men bought. Some sold.
Some loaded horses onto trailers
and drove away. Would the horses go
to slaughter? Would they end up at the track?
Horses of different dispositions, breeding,
conformation. Horses of various sizes, of
each sex. Though I wore a buckle,
the cowboys knew I was just a girl
in a place of men. The auctioneer's gavel
struck and struck.

My Horse Had the On-Screen Persona of James Dean

We picked up a canter to round the ring.
Young riders on frisky ponies,
preteens on lumbering horses
and all kinds of horses in between.
Too close, and a kick could fly out.

I tried to keep a distance. You could
already see who would be losing. The winners
were harder to tell apart. A teen carried in
the ribbons. The judge marked the clipboard
and called the numbers to step forward. My horse
rested one leg. He was like the cool boy in class

who didn't want to pay attention. He swatted
flies, tried to reach down to eat. I was so glad
when the announcer called my number. But then my horse
didn't want to move. I urged and urged, and he put one hoof
in front of the other so slowly I thought they'd take back
the ribbon, thought the judge would rethink her math.
But the class was over. The horse could do what he wanted.

As soon as we walked through the gate, I jumped off, pulled
the reins over his head, and led him far from the ring,
back to the trailer, where I slipped the halter on and he
stomped and bent to graze, moving his lips continually
over the land, as if he had never eaten grass before.

Remote

The discos on Route 22,
in 1979, when mirrored balls
flashed with the throbbing
base. We grabbed each
other's arms, hustled back
and forth between steps. It
was easy to be as free as
a whirlwind, the teenage
night twinkling with its
own lights. You're 60
now, hair as long as then,
body as spry. You'd
gallop on a horse any day,
and I'd watch you ride
fast into the clutches
of the relentless night.
How did it happen, this
pulse into quickening age?
How did it seem as if it would
never end? Your father ready
at the head of the table,
his strong hands on the
table, then on the arms
of the chair. Your mother
stirring the spaghetti. You,
opening the fridge for drinks,
the first string in a subtle
harmony. Even your
horses danced in the upper
pastures, as if sensing
the tones. Even the cat
that was usually sleeping
lifted her head in rhythm
with your movement
through the door. I think
the farm was blessed.
I could tell when your

mother gathered the coats
from the front closet.
I felt she was lifting all
our troubles off and into
the crisp country air for
varmints to devour. This
was the hour for goodbyes.
The road like a pinwheel
to the carnival sky.

1:05 PM Train Whistle

At least it's midday, its whistle-whistle,
rumble-rumble a quarter mile away,
my suburban lifestyle interrupted

by a reminder of America moving ahead.
Train from the past, let me see your cross-
country rails, your decades wobbling from

side to side. Let me reimagine hobo life
of the 30s, settling the West. I booked a room
on a sleeper of a Southern Railway train in 1975.

I had a nostalgia for trains. I rode the Northeast Corridor in 1978 to 9, waited in line
at the Princeton Junction station, looking

out for the express to New York City,
willing to switch to subway to subway
in the caverns of Manhattan to rise

into the skyscraper light of day. All along
that train route: the homes of suburbs, once
rural New Jersey, cow pastures and small business,

high fences and motor vehicles. Platforms
at Linden, Rahway, Metuchen. The big Newark
swallowing us. I dreamed to the top of the Empire

State, the towers of the World Trade Center.
One could do almost anything in New York City.
Finger of the world. Pointed pleasures.

All from the shimmying of the train.
Crawling into the black of rock island
to its escape. I had a dream of where

the train could take me and where
it had been. I found myself a part of
the train, reveling in its clang and puff

and relentlessness. Now it's an echo
through the last pastures, a surprise
as its cars pass over bridges, and shrink

in the distance in a tunnel of trees
fanning out to parceled land, numbers
of people hurrying up.

Spring Romp

In the upper pasture, a stiff breeze,
and the mares buck, shaking their heads,
    their manes as shiny as the manes of young fillies.

A few colts in the neighboring field catch wind of it and break
into a canter, baring their teeth at one another's sides.
    Just moments before, all was quiet.

I was brushing my gelding on the crossties.
Just moments ago, I was putting the tack away
    before I stopped to watch the horses graze on one of the few

estates left in this part of New Jersey. I began
to think that it must have been like this fifty years ago.
    And suddenly, at fifty, I too would like to take a spring romp,

because right now the horses are kicking it up in the grazed-
    off pasture near the spring-risen brook by the over-
whelming elm, American oak, and towering pine.

Writing by Hand

Once,
people wrote long letters, pages
long. You could see the emotion in
the loops, in the tilt of the script, in
the darkness of the ink. Stationery
was personal. People often bought stationery
embossed with their initials or with designs
in the borders. You wouldn't just

sign your name as people do now with a greeting
card. And you would wait to get a letter back,
checking the mailbox every day, asking the postman.
No, nothing for you today. You knew the postman
because he delivered your personal letters
and usually on foot. He'd park down the street and carry

the mail over a block or so. He'd come right up to your house.
We had a mailbox at eye level next to the front door. He
had to walk down a path and climb up steps to the porch
to reach it. It had a little loop underneath for magazines
and newspapers. Some people also had slots in their doors that
the mailman could slide the mail into. I don't remember

when all that changed, when you had
to put your mailbox on the street so
the mailman could drive to it. I didn't know my
mailman after that, only by sight. And people stopped
writing letters so much, until it was rare to get a handwritten letter at all,
which leads me to writing by hand and how penmanship
was taught and learned, and how you would comment on how
unique or beautiful or illegible someone's handwriting was. Now
you usually do that only with a signature.
And does a signature count anyway?
I don't know if I could handwrite a letter again. I'm so encouraged
by speed these days. Handwriting is a leisure activity, meaning
you relax into it. Yet I wish everyone would go back

to handwriting at least once in a while. Something about it
makes you reveal, plunder the heart's complexities.
I'd even go back to inkwell and fountain pen
at least once a year. It could be an event. We could see
what the body meant through the motion of the hand.

Condo Morning in the Suburbs

The rumble rolls under my bed and up
into my ear. It's not the cricket chirp or
the bird call I expected. It's not the gentle light

parting my curtains, but cigarette wafts drifting
in. As a child, I never dreamed of condo life.
I lived in a house with my own room shaded

by an old pine that was taller than the house.
Its thick branches reached like arms, and beneath them
lay a bed of needles with pinecones we used for decorating

come fall. The yard was grassy too, and we slid
down the hill to the sidewalk in winter
when new snow made us pull out pieces

of cardboard for sleds, which were light
and worked better on our makeshift mountain.
But here, there are no hills. And kids pretty much

play in the horseshoe street of the parking lot,
though there's a yard out back. There's even a pine
tree. But there's no skateboard ramp. There's no

basketball hoop. A car rolls in with its beat-thumping.
A door slams. The trash container lid comes ramming down,
echoing throughout the court. When silence comes,

it's like a long lost meadow breathing. It's like New
Jersey in 1960, when things were just beginning
to get a little congested. A neighbor's voice could

be heard calling her kids. A telephone ring could
carry through an open window. *Is that
ours?* The suburb: a community endeavor.

If your kid was bad, a neighbor scolded him and
told you. And then you reprimanded him and apologized
to the neighbor. A kid rarely talked back to an adult.

It's easy to think things were better before, because
the past leaves the taste of a metal spoon off of
the ice cream. Still, it seems the slam-boom-

and-bang of *now* reverberates off buildings, and
"Good morning" is rare in the rush of door-to-car-
and-go. My condo morning is a dream of yesteryear

backed up down the highway. If only we could find
another way home. I touch my global positioning
device, and it gives me alternate routes. I'd like to take

a back road, but it takes too long. I wonder what we did
when we didn't know where we were, when we had
to look for a gas station, like a crossroad, or a phone booth

that could connect you to the world, *your* world. I could
move my condo to almost any suburb anywhere and eventually
find my way around a nearby strip mall or a superstore. "Good

morning, America." Let me fly out of my condo door, so like
every other door in my domino of buildings. *Tweet-tweet.*
Let's get something to eat. *Whack* goes the door.

At the Shore
—c. 2007

The ocean smells of landfill.
I sense erosion.
But look at the eyes of the child
waiting in line. We've

bought tickets for rides. We all know
our way around the funhouse of
mirrors, and the flume with rushing
water rounds only once.

The boardwalk buoys me up.
I wish the beach didn't smell
dredged. I wish the air were still
taffy-sweet. I wish that I

were a child again, because
I'd never leave. My future
would be sunburnt, as sunny
as a shiny wooden pony. I

would stay on for another ride,
my life belonging to no other time.
I'd hop astride a gold-flecked steed,
music blasting out a mesmeric rhythm.

Building for Books

Reverence,
though only three syllables,
seems longer, nails down
the tongue just before the end.
We have to be quiet. *Shh!* We have to

still our bodies in reverence to
the stillness of books. *Shh.*
One page, *swoosh.* Then another.
Our eyes focused on the book.
Imagine the architect's dream to

house the book. Surely, the book
must contain something we want,
something nearly as vital as breath,
which flows toward the book.
Here, we have to borrow the book.

The book, sacred as sharing.
The book, no matter how old, holds
light. Just as light pours into the building,
as if within us, so too does the light of the book.
That's why we want to write the book,

to see that light and let it surface,
out of ourselves. Temple of light. Sacred
word. Myth of the father. I pray in the library
of my own heart. *Shh.* God is hovering.
The bread of Christ, like a page in the book,

paper/wafer-like. I eat the pages of my book.
But "No, don't," says the librarian. So I sit still,
like a schoolgirl who listens. I look around,
see that others are obeying the rules. Wonder
what they're learning in all of those books,

wonder if they should run with the books,
feeling the exhilaration of light. Footsteps . . .
I look up. You can't avoid footsteps. On the hard
floor of the library, above which the books float.
The pages, like bird-wing feathers.

The Rest Stop

Will there always be rest stops? Fifty years ago, they were where you could make a telephone call from a public phone, put a dime down for a soda, maybe have a donut, coffee, or scrambled eggs.

You said hello to strangers at rest stops, asked them where they were going. You were happy to have made it to a rest stop, because you didn't want to have to use the side of the road with your car door open or bushes in a field to hide you.

Now when cars start to drive themselves, will you ask them to go to a rest stop if you have to use the restroom, which is where you rarely rest?—but you never take a bath in a bathroom with no bath either and certainly not at a rest stop.

Will there be no need for rest stops, as everything will have sped up so much that some other means of handling bodily functions will have evolved? It seems so mechanical already. Who knows you, or seems to want to, or dares not for many reasons all too peculiar to list?

Time was, most people wanted to know something about you if you wanted to tell. Time was, you saw that rest stop and were relieved even before you entered the building.

Making Our Best Life

Bizzzz. Morning jolts the way.
Not the rooster. Not the slow sunrise. Oh, why another day tied

to the desk? Rise, fool! Make your life.
Everyone has a job till death. Otherwise,
your obituary will bleed. Routinize.

Are you also working nine to five? Give me
shelter. Let me dine on filet mignon.
Lay me down on thousand-thread-count sheets

ordered from TV. Little moments
run up to you. What to do?
What false move will grab you? And

do you really care? Commute. Compute.
Construct. The past is rolling down
the road and waving. The living

have a spoon in their mouths. Everyone
wants to be fed. I can't believe the dead
are not looking at me when my future's

shrinking into a ball small enough
to hold. Is this the earth I'm looking at?
Is this my life? No matter what bed

we sleep in, we all wake facing
the day proportionate to what we want.
After dinner, what shall we watch?

Why can't words keep me awake?
Is there nothing I need to say?
Now that the hour closes in on me,

shall I dream? *I am your finest
nightmare*, says my ego. And
I am too tired to respond.

Dust

lodges in your mouth—it
    tastes old, and sweet at the same
        time—time itself must taste
            like this

as it starts counting down
    your life. How do you mark
        your existence?
            The fat cow of you grazing

in the heartland of America. I am singing
    that song on the lip of a prayer I
        once believed in, to a God
            who left me when I

hitched a ride in a boxcar with
    plush seating and the con-
        ductor really didn't care if I got
            off at the next stop without paying.

I'm counting down, America. How long
    have you got for me? Why
        are you running so, charging on
            like a freight train?

Give me your colicky blues.
    Make my stop-to-change-trains
        the District of Columbia grass-
            land, not a beggar in sight,

because he's still in that boxcar.
    You taste what he tastes.
        You feel the past
            like a multi-colored word that's

no longer correct. Dump out your grave
    diggers, America. Leave your gang
        wielding pistols to kill our inner
            cities. We're living on the out-

skirts anyhow, and we don't welcome
    outsiders. The truth is twisted and washed
        clean in the suburbs. Go ahead.
            Your survival depends on it.

Leave no child behind, or several
    who'll come looking for you when
        you're gone, riding that boxcar
            through fields of grass, up-ended.

Summer

has overdone itself, has out-
done its sweltering. Parched
America sells her cattle, and
food prices soar. It's a brutal

week in the Midwest. And no storms.
Not the summer quenchers of
yesteryear come to pummel and flood.
No one wants to go out in the rains.

Even the night crawlers stay underground. And punks have lost their marshy
homes to grow. Kids are reluctant to
get up early, run a paper route, or sell

lemonade outside all day, which now
requires a permit. They're used to air
conditioning and video games. They're
used to being driven everywhere.

If the bull is thirsty, they don't know it.
If the land cracks, we'll turn
the sprinklers on. If God needs a prayer,
we can always bring out the tuning fork.

In a Minute

The wise.
    The unwise.
        All slap themselves,

clasp their hands together.
    The Arizona sun hovers
        over the rattlesnake.

You listen. The earth is cracked.
    And thirsty. You're looking
        for water. But there's only

a heat wave, the mirage
    of direction staring
        at you so hard

you turn around. Don't bet
    on a sunset. It's too
        sentimental, and sentiment

is *out*. Better to lie
    and keep yourself silly.
        Who cares? We're too

busy with our lives.
    The soil of the desert
        surfaces in Nebraska,

then in New York City. It surfaces
    in your home in the suburbs,
        where everyone is the same

as they were supposed to be.
     Your "block" is a lesson
          in sociology. A multiple-

choice test. You can guess,
      you know. It's graded on
         a curve. And everyone passes.

I've forgotten the beginning of my life,
      the conception of a minute.
         Wait a minute. Stop

for a minute.

Dress Shop

The dress shop I used to visit as a girl has moved into one small room
the size of a coffee shop, items packed onto racks placed catty-corner—

to save space?—or into glass cases as if relics from another era.
A woman buzzes open the door. A car drives up; its loud music

vibrates through the store. At the bus stop, an elderly man stoops over,
waiting. Curteous, I browse the racks. A dog follows me—

wants to be petted, the woman explains. Wedding dresses take up
one rack—dresses that used to have their own department, almost

as large as this store. Mother would receive news of the new season's
clothes. We'd talk of buying items from New York and Paris.

It was possible to believe in such fantasy. *No, thank you,* I tell
the woman, who starts pulling out purses to sell to me. Before,

I'd have to ask, and the salesgirl would eventually wait on me,
as if she didn't *have* to sell anything. I make my way

to the door. And the woman buzzes it open. I slip through
the rush of air and onto the pavement of a strip mall.

Subscribing in the Suburbs

Where are the comics online?
There's a lot I miss.
Read fast. Skim the world.

Sooner or later, you admit
you miss the feel of the paper,
the way you lost yourself inside

it as you held it with both
hands and pulled it close
to read the whole story, how

it changed you, like a good book
that someone had taken the time
to research. Now you're

in the suburbs. Half-gas,
half-electric, hybrid
of the next century.

En Route to See You at the Jersey Shore

33—that long semi-rural stretch
to the Jersey Shore, north of Seaside,

where Victorian homes pyramid to rise
out of turn-of-the-century America with

clapboard and billowing flags, salt and sea
on the tourist's tongue. En route

to see you, we suddenly begin to jolt in our
ten-year-old four-door, which never gives us

any problems. We stop at an old gas station
that's closed. I pull out my cell phone,

fumble for the slip of paper I wrote
your number on. We pop the hood,

look around, fiddle with this and that,
as neither of us knows much about cars.

We stall and start, stall and start,
and leave you a message—you who are

probably looking out a window to the beach,
a vista I too long to see. You probably

already have some sun on your face, some
warmth in your body from the relaxation and

the nostalgia of the surroundings that
you knew as a child. I too want

to go there, to see you both smile
and hear you laugh that child-

laughter that knows not to grow up. We could
have gulped some of that sea air, could

have consumed fine food and good wine.
I'm sorry—we're sorry. But can we make it

another time? I don't know when.
We stall and start, stall and start all the way

back from the halfway-mark-to-you
to the hills of central New Jersey, where

highways and streets connect the suburbs
to the next city, with greenery in between.

I hope we get to see you next time.
I hope so many years don't pass.

Good morning . . .

Rumble-rumble, the earth's muscle.
Night: a low-light canvas. Nothing to be expected
at 5 a.m., other than odd creepings in the bones,
off-dream wanderings. You said tomorrow
would come with taffy, that we would board
the merry-go-round at Seaside, where painted
horses twisted their necks in delicatory surprise,
where you could see the lone ring that attended
everyone's wishes. We'd smell cotton candy,
hear the game-men hawk their wares,
with promise teetering on the arrow of a wheel.
Tick tick tick. Where would it stop? Who would win
or lose? Who would walk down the boardwalk
with that stuffed animal you once admired and
coveted, because it meant you could actually have
what seemed out of reach? The ocean air curled
around corners. You could smell it, even taste its salt
on your lips. The muffled sounds of action,
of approach and retreat. I held the ear of the future
to mine. There were rumblings I could not decipher.
There were long re-turns, someone driving the snake
road through the Pine Barrens, pine and chill filling
the air. We passed the lake roads where Aunt lived.
We passed the Russian Orthodox church and the dance hall
where men danced the kazatsky. It seemed that distance
was squeezing the past, that we would one day forget
how to partner to feel the rhythms of the day.
It wasn't necessary to be old, or decrepit, as
the carousel fifty years later would not be, but
splendid in the searching horses still longing to
round the center musical cylinder where the man
to take your ticket would suddenly appear.
If not for the music and the insistent circling,
would we have wanted to get off? Would we
have wanted to leave, with Mother's continuing
smiles and Dad's waiting with the world
in his arms? No wonder we spotted the soft-serve

stand at the center of the boardwalk and stared as
the teenage girls and boys swirled what we wanted
into cones and cups. And we ate the coolness like
diving into a wave that would splash onto the beach
behind us. We had met our delight when we could
claim it. We all walked on, the night with its pearly
sky casting a grey sheen against the lights. The white
caps breaking, the sand still between our toes no matter
how long we wiped our feet. A speck here or there the ocean
deposited. You didn't know when. You didn't know when
it would be your last time there, despite those stories of
Mother's father on the movable bench, looking
out to sea while the children played. What was he dreaming
that couldn't have been found someday?
Or was it just a dream with no past recognizable to greet
us again? Maybe he knew Russia was gone. His home
was a line on a map someone else had claimed. His past
was an ocean away, and he had roller-bearing grease
on his arm. How he'd never go back. How the future
was a store of his own. Sometimes, Grandmother
would give small bags of candy to children, as if gifts
from some magical place where the music kept playing
while the horses arched their necks and pranced.

ACKNOWLEDGMENTS

Crab Orchard Review, "From the 22nd Floor" (originally published as "From the 21st Floor")

Earth's Daughters, "The lake, when I was growing up,"

Interdisciplinary Humanities, "Subscribing in the Suburbs" (previous version)

Mothers and Sons: Centering Mother Knowledge (Demeter Press, 2016), "The Fast"

You Are Here: New York City Streets in Poetry (P & Q Press, 2006), "On the Edge of a City"

Tokens: Contemporary Poetry of the Subway (P & Q Press, 2003), "Manhattan," "From a Rooftop in Brooklyn"

Unruly Catholic Women Writers: Creative Responses to Catholicism (Excelsior Editions/SUNY Press, 2013), "Saying Penance" (previous version, originally published as "Penance")

Whitefish Review, "Raccoon Prints"

SPECIAL THANKS

With many thanks to my mother, Dolores J. Stark, for her love and stories. Thanks to Rudolph R. Stark for bringing New Jersey history alive. Much appreciation to Molly Peacock for her support and guidance over the years. Thank you to Nancy and Edward Smoller for their friendship and support. Thanks to Lynn Harrison-Pope for her friendship and to Aunt Teresa for her generous hospitality during my many visits and stays "in the country" of New Jersey. And, of course, deep appreciation and love to my husband, Dennis, for his love, support, and keen editing.

Special thanks to Dr. Leslie Kreiner Wilson for the generous time to complete this manuscript and to the Board of Directors of Americana, the Advisory Board of *Review Americana*, and the Editor of Press Americana, Dr. Wilson, for selecting this manuscript for the Prize Americana for Poetry.

ABOUT THE AUTHOR

Donna J. Gelagotis Lee earned a B.A., cum laude, in English and creative writing from Sweet Briar College, where she was a Davison-Foreman scholar. She is the author of *On the Altar of Greece* (Gival Press, 2006), winner of the Gival Press Poetry Award and recipient of a 2007 Eric Hoffer Book Award: Notable for Art Category. Her poetry has appeared internationally in literary and scholarly journals, including *The Bitter Oleander, The Cortland Review, Feminist Studies, Journal of New Jersey Poets, The Massachusetts Review, Review Americana*, and *Women's Studies Quarterly*. Her website is www.donnajgelagotislee.com.

Made in the USA
Middletown, DE
16 February 2019